# Enjoy the
# 5G Network of GOD

**…Infinitely more breathtaking than anyone can comprehend!**

*A Powerful 31 Day Program*

*to Tap into & FEAST on GOD's 5G Network!*

By

## Gerard Assey Ph.D

# Enjoy the 5G Network of GOD

By Gerard Assey

Copyright © 2020 by Gerard Assey

# Table of Contents

# Dedication

This book that you have in your hands is dedicated to all those who would like to FEAST on and Taste GOD's true nature…

*"Oh, taste and see that the LORD is good; Blessed is the man who trusts in Him!*

*Psalms 34.8*

# Living and Enjoying a 5G Life!

Have you ever thought how people communicated till around 30 years ago? If you are in your forties or later, then there is a sure chance that your parents transferred information manually if they had to communicate with someone overseas. They would write a letter that would take 3 to 4 months to get across to the addressed person on the other side of the world. That was called the 'snail age'.

As time went by, we got into what we called the 'email age' and from there the world eventually graduated from 2G to 3G and then to 4 G and now we are talking of 5G- the G standing for Generation of wireless technology.

With most of us in the possession of a cell phone we are certainly familiar with the terms 3G and 4G already and some even with 5G terminology. They refer to various generations of data connections. Each new generation of phone works faster and allows the user to do more on their cell phone. As we all know, the 5G has already begun to stir a lot of controversy especially after the onset of COVID-19. But on the other hand the 5G is claimed to be the fastest form of internet ever with a number of benefits to daily life-in business and on the personal front. According to experts 5G will be as much as 100 times faster than the current 4G cellular networks. It will transform the way we work, learn, communicate, and travel. While all this is on the positive side of this technology, a panel of scientists recently published a warning of the potential health risks that pervasive electromagnetic field (EMF) exposure may bring- and the list is huge. (Since that's not the objective of this book, I am not getting into them). What we need to note however is that, as technology becomes more and more a part of our everyday lives, it could change our perspective of how things could possibly play out in the next few years.

The good news is that we as Christians have a much better 5G life to enjoy that sadly many have not tapped into! A better connection to

God! When we connect through God's 5G network, we are assured of what He promises in John 10.10: *"I came that you may have life and have it more abundantly."* These are Jesus' words- His promise to you and me. Just as how the service provider offering you the 5G connection assures you of a host of services, yet we know from all our experiences that despite the so-called best plans- we are still let down at some time or the other. But we have in this promise coming from none other than the one involved in creation- (John 1:1-3, Revelation 19:13) –the Son of GOD-Jesus Himself, who said *"I came that you may have life and have it more abundantly"* A connectivity with no disruption! A promise that can never be broken; and a promise that stands for life!

The word abundantly is from a Greek word that means *over and above, more than is necessary, superior, extraordinary, surpassing, uncommon.* Now given this, we as believers are to then have an extraordinary 5G connection to God in some way or the other, but yet sadly our lives are very much like the rest of the world. We still do not feel that we are living this extraordinary, bountiful and supernatural life that is flowing with the abundance of peace, joy and wholeness that the Word of God promises.

So how do we get a life like that then? Let's first look at what happens when life begins to throw challenges at us. Immediately our view of God's presence and all that He has provided around us can become cloudy, as we start to question: *'If God is good, why is there so much evil and suffering?'* In times like this, it's so easy to lose sight of God's many blessings and gifts. But at the door of your heart, God waits patiently and desires for you to open up to a relationship with Him- a relationship that will enable you understand Him deeper. He has prepared a feast for you even in the presence of the difficulties and challenges you are facing, and God wants you to be able to enjoy that abundant life He has provided, not just survive it.

That's where the 5G's of God (not of this world) come in. In 5G terms they are HIS **Goodness**, HIS **Greatness**, HIS **Glory**, HIS

Grace and HIS **Gifts**. These are the signals that connect us to tap into and FEAST on the abundant life GOD has promised for us. How do we connect to those signals and tap into this 5G life is what this book will hopefully help you do.

**'Enjoy the 5G Network of God'** is not just another Christian self-help book, though it will help you do that too. It is not a complete bible study, though you will still learn a lot about the Creator. It is not designed to motivate you to try harder, though you will also be motivated. It does not contain the steps to achieve personal success, though when you begin to feast and taste God's 5G's, you WILL find a sense of joy, peace and wholeness filling you. Additionally, this 31 Day Powerful Program does offer practical ways that can be used individually, or in groups, or for an entire church family to make living in His goodness your everyday reality- enabling you to tap into and FEAST on GOD's 5G Network!

Finally, when you taste God's 5G's, you will be impacted with everything you see around you. And as you experience this 5G life, your Heart will start to FEAST and respond in total Gratitude!

I pray that this little booklet be a Blessing to you and many others!

# The Goodness of God

Almost every Christian knows that song by Don Moen, *'God is Good all the time...'* with almost every church singing it sometime or the other- that God IS good. But what does that mean—that God is *good*?

The more we study His word in the Bible, the more one central concept seems to jump out: God's goodness conveys His heart of generosity. His goodness means far more than His generosity, but it certainly includes His infinitely generous attitude toward us. By nature, He longs to bring joy and blessing to all His creatures. All through the Bible, we find that it repeatedly presents goodness as a core quality of our Lord. The Bible reveals that goodness is part of God's essential nature. When we say that God is good, it means that which is in the nature and character of God that causes Him to be kind and benevolent. By His inherent nature He takes pleasure in bestowing blessings and happiness on His people. That is what Psalms 119.68 reiterates: *"He is good and He does good.*

In the beginning He made the universe and behold, it was very good! Everything that He does is still very good. Since the Almighty is immutable, His goodness can never change in the slightest way. He will never be better than He is now, nor will He ever be any less good. Since God is infinite, perfect and eternal, His goodness is boundless and can never cease. Everything that He will ever do will always be good. No human will ever be able to comprehend the full extent of God's goodness. He has unending goodness in store for us.

Some people assume that God is only good to those who are good to Him, but that is not true. God's goodness is not restricted to believers alone – oh no! *The Lord is good <u>to all</u>, and His mercies are over all of His works* (Psalm 145:9). Paul's message to even the pagans of Lystra was that *God did not leave Himself without witness, in that He did good and gave you rains from heaven and fruitful seasons, satisfying your hearts with food and gladness*

(Acts 14:17). Jesus when teaching his disciples told them that *"… He causes His sun to shine on the evil and the good, and He sends rain on the righteous and the unrighteous* (Matthew. 5:45).

In Psalm 145 David calls us to take the time to look back on our lives and reflect on the goodness of our God. We are encouraged to praise God for His greatness, His mercy and compassion, His faithfulness, and to thank God for His many gifts that we've received all throughout our lives. In the words of that old hymn, we are urged to, *"Count your blessings, name them one by one."*

But maybe when you look back on this year or certain stages in your life you may feel you were not blessed at all. And because of this, it's possible that you may not feel like praising God. You may be saying, "It's ok for you, but there is absolutely nothing that I could possibly be thankful for." Perhaps life came to you in ways you never anticipated. But the Word of God promises, that in spite of everything that happens in our lives, God never leaves us. And to demonstrate this love for us, He gave us the greatest gift imaginable, the gift of His only begotten Son, the Lord Jesus. And when we have Him, what more do we need. That answers it all. As Paul says in Romans 8:32, *"He who did not spare His own Son, but gave Him up for us all—how will He not also, along with Him, graciously give us all things?"*

For you to truly get a hold of this truth you first need to grasp the fact that God deeply loves you  and He is sovereign over every situation. He is not a bad God who wants you to constantly live in fear. Those fearful and anxious thoughts come only from Satan. God wants His children to be joyful. If we are broken today, then our brokenness attributes to our broken view of God- nothing else!

Right from the beginning of time, God has been in the business of building the love relationship between us and Him and helping us to see who He is. God is in the business of setting you free from those thoughts that keep you captive. You don't have to wake up every morning thinking that He is trying to hurt you. No, He is good, He cares for you, and He loves you. Do you believe that He is good? Don't just sing songs about His goodness. This study will help you get to understand what God being good truly means.

The best part is that God's goodness never ends! God doesn't just stop being good. Don't think to yourself, "I messed up this week and I know God is going to get me." This is such a broken view of God. We mess up every day, but God is continually pouring out His endless grace and mercy upon us. His goodness is not dependent on you, but it's dependent on who He is. God, by nature, is inherently good. So does God allow trials to happen? Yes, but even when He does allow these things He is still good and worthy of praise. We can be confident that we serve a God who will work good things out of bad situations. Now don't get me wrong; I know life can be so difficult. So many questions are left unanswered on your mind, but the Word of God reminds us as Christians, that we are called to come back to the good. What is good? God is. End of story.

We have to know that in all things, he is working it out. The only option is to trust, have faith, and surrender our end game for His **After all this said, do you still have any doubt that God is good?** Try Him out! *Taste and see that the Lord is good* (Psalm 34:8). And you will discover what the Psalmist did when he declared that *the nearness of God is my good* (Psalm 73:28). As you begin to renew your mind reading and meditating on the rest of this book about the goodness of God, your confidence in His goodness and love for you will soar! Begin expecting to see manifestations of the goodness of God in your life-Every. Single. Day! So live in this confidence today and the rest of your days that the giving God is always with you.

# The Greatness of God

The word 'greatness' is found 37 times in the Old and New Testament with the Bible revealing a God so great that we cannot compare anything even close to Him. But we can still learn a lot by meditating on the power and greatness of this God.

Let us look at what God has to say about Himself. In Isaiah 40:15-17 God says, *"Behold, the nations are as a drop in a bucket, and are counted as the small dust on the scales; look, He lifts up the isles as a very little thing. And Lebanon is not sufficient to burn, nor its beasts sufficient for a burnt offering. All nations before Him are as nothing, and they are counted by Him less than nothing and worthless."* Despite what God says, we yet find that many still do not understand the greatness of God. God goes on to say in verses 18-19, *"To whom then will you liken God? Or what likeness will you compare to Him? The workman molds an image, the goldsmith overspreads it with gold, and the silversmith casts silver chains."* Because none of us have seen God, God tells us here that whatever we do or make, nothing can come anywhere even close to revealing who He is. Yet we see many images and statues that are supposed to be representations of God in the world today, even though the Scriptures warn us that we should not make an image of God. Why? Because it is impossible for us to truly get the right picture of the power and glory of this great God in our physical state that we are in. The other and most important reason is that God being a Spirit, we relate to Him only in Spirit and in truth (John 4:23, 24)

Scriptures tell us clearly that no human was allowed to see God in His glorified state, though God did reveal Himself in the form of a man. When Moses had requested to see God in His glory, God replied, *"You cannot see My face; for no man shall see Me, and live"* (Exodus 33:20). Moses, who was a faithful prophet of God, was only allowed to see God's back (verse 23).

So how can we then truly come to understand this great God and His glorious attributes? One way to understand more about God's greatness and glory is to study His incredible characteristics through the world that we live in. The apostle Paul said in Romans 1:20, that God's glory and power are shown in the physical creation: *"For since the creation of the world His invisible attributes are clearly seen, being understood by the things that are made, even His eternal power and Godhead, so that they are without excuse"* Notice that the physical world shows *"His invisible attributes."* By looking at the world and the universe, we can get only a fraction of an inkling of the incredible power and glory of God. What scientists, researchers and astronomers have found are only a drop in the ocean of His marvelous creation and wonder. The more scientists look into life, the more complexity they find. Even the "simple" cell is extremely complex. The more scientists discover about the universe, the more spectacular and awe-inspiring we find it to be. David said, *"The heavens declare the glory of God; and the firmament shows His handiwork"*-Psalm 19:1. That is why Paul goes on further to extol God's greatness in Romans 11:33: *"Oh, the depth of the riches both of the wisdom and knowledge of God! How unsearchable are His judgments and His ways past finding out!"*

Proverbs 3:19 states: *"The LORD by wisdom founded the earth; by understanding He established the heavens."* God's ways are so much different from the ways of man that His wisdom goes far beyond our understanding, and He often works in ways that we do not understand. That is why God says in Isaiah 55:8-9, *"For My thoughts are not your thoughts, nor are your ways My ways,' says the LORD. 'For as the heavens are higher than the earth, so are My ways higher than your ways, and My thoughts than your thoughts."*

God's ways are much superior to our ways. Paul talks of that in 1 Corinthians 2:9, *"Eye has not seen, nor ear heard, nor have entered into the heart of man the things which God has prepared for those who love Him."* God's plan and promises are unbelievingly good which includes a time of peace, prosperity, goodness, wholeness and eternal life for us that they cannot be fully described in human terms.

Now the question is: Do you find God great and greatly to be praised? Is He worthy of your adoration, honor and daily praise? Do you think enough *of* Him or *about* Him that it results in you telling Him how much you love Him? God's greatness is unsearchable. In other words, you could never plumb the depths of His greatness. Just when you think you know how great God is, He surprises you. God's greatness isn't limited or exhaustible. He doesn't run out of wonders or miracles to perform. God is sovereign and ruler over everyone and everything. God's word is final.

Our problem is that we allow our minds to be occupied with thoughts of anything and everything but God, including ourselves. We end up praising all kinds of things but God, who alone is worthy of our praise. Every day we wake up, we should offer Him the praise, honor and gratitude He so richly deserves. And no matter how often we praise Him, we will never run out of praiseworthy things for which to honor Him.

# The Glory of God

Before we get into understanding God's glory we would first need to look at what the term *'glory'* actually means. Like many other theological concepts, God's glory is a concept that we have an awareness of without necessarily being able to describe it in all its fullness. The Glory of God also known as Shekinah glory- the Hebrew name, isn't just a feeling, an event or an Old Testament experience- it's a spiritual tsunami of everything contained in the character of God. It has been called the manifested presence of God, but more than just a presence, it is power.

When we think of the glory of the Lord, the image of brilliant light often comes to our minds. That is certainly appropriate, as Scripture often describes the glory of God in terms of a light that shines brighter than anything that we experience on earth. For example, we see in Isaiah 60.1-3 and in Revelation 21:22–25, the glory of our Creator and not the sun being the light that shines forth in this dark world, revealing itself through God's people that they might point the pagan nations unto the Lord of all, tells us that in the new heaven and earth, creation will have no need for the sun by day or the moon by night because the glory of the Lord shall illumine all of creation.

When we look straight into the sun, its brilliance can be blinding, but the beautiful, clear light radiating from the sun also helps us see the things around us. Sunlight also radiates heat, warming the earth each day as it gives light for plants and for growing food. We cannot separate the radiating light and heat from the sun; these properties always go together with sunlight for our life here on earth.

Similarly, we cannot separate Jesus, the Son of God, from God Himself. Hebrews says, *"The Son is the radiance of God's glory. . . ."* Think about what this means: in Jesus, the *glory of God* came to dwell among us, taking on our flesh and becoming one of us. The glory of God in Christ was humbled on the cross when He died to pay the price of our sin for us. Then the glory of God shone in its brilliance when Jesus rose again from the dead. *"The radiance of God's glory"* came for all to see. As the gospel of John explains in John 1.9, Jesus came to give light to everyone in the world. Jesus came to draw us to Himself, the light of the world, so that we could come out of darkness.

The glory of God, which is manifested in all His attributes altogether, never passes away. It is eternal. The kind of power that resurrects, delivers, overcomes and transforms, is greater and stronger than any other power in existence. And it belongs to us. But, if we aren't expecting to see the glory of God, we won't. It takes faith to see a manifestation. Can you see physical manifestations of God's glory today? When was the last time you stopped and considered the glory of God? What other persons or things compete for the affection of your heart? Can you think of a time when the glory led you to experience awe, which led you to worship God?

# The Grace of God

God is known to be a God of 'Mercy and Grace' with the word grace found 138 times in the Old and New Testament. Grace can be a tough concept to grasp. God is often described as gracious, but what does that mean for us? We sing about it, we read about it, and we talk about it- we use this word loosely. But do we really understand it?

Many of us operate under the assumption that God's grace is like human grace — imperfect, exchange-based, reactive, and subject to change. We feel the pressure to earn grace, and we have an enemy who wants to keep it that way. We begin thinking God owes us salvation because of our excellent church attendance or charity and giving record. Or we believe God owes us an economically stable life because we aren't "bad" like everyone else. But the Bible is clear that grace is a gift, purchased by Jesus' death on the cross and given to us freely out of God's love for us. God's grace, His undeserved favor, is not a reward for human effort. God's grace is based entirely on who He is and who we are in Him. God gives us grace because He wants to. By grace, we are adopted into His family, our debts paid and our sin forgiven. It is His pleasure and will to give us these things when we put our faith in Jesus and believe in His finished work for us. No one can take away or lessen the power of this supernatural exchange. When we truly experience God's grace, we cannot help but be drawn to the One who gives it to us, enabling us to worry less about messing up and now focusing more on getting to know the God who loves us. The reality of our situation is this: we, "His workmanship", created in Christ Jesus for good works", owe God everything, while He owes us nothing! We are saved by grace "through faith" in Jesus; and don't forget, even our confession of faith is due to the Holy Spirit's work in our hearts (1 Corinthians 12:3)! So as you meditate today, pray that the Holy Spirit would reveal any pride concerning your salvation and inherent goodness that ought not to be. God is merciful to even the worst offenders, sinners and lawbreakers. This means that even though He knows of our guilt, in His mercy, He does not dispense the full consequences of what we deserve, and in His grace, He blesses us with many good gifts in spite of what we have done, giving us what we do not deserve. All of this reflects the fact that, *'God demonstrates His own love for us in this: While we were still sinners, Christ died for us.'* Instead of giving us what we deserve, God has shown mercy again and again, not to take away our responsibility, but to give us a chance.

What we can sum up about Grace is that it is an unmerited favor, an undeserved love, and an apt description of God's interaction with mankind. This sets us apart from every other "religion" on the face of the earth. This is astounding when we properly understand even a little bit about who is dealing graciously with us.

What if we stopped exhausting ourselves trying to earn God's favor and simply asked Him to help us see and receive what is already ours to rest in? How different would life be?

As undeserving recipients of God's mercy, nothing else would be more fitting than that we just THANK AND PRAISE HIM all the days of our lives!

# The Gifts of God

At most times we think of gifts when it comes to birthdays, weddings and other special occasions, and if we are to make a list, it might include a high-end mobile phone, a diamond or gold bracelet, or even a greeting card full of cash. Who wouldn't want or like a tangible display of affection, especially if it was a bit expensive? Yet when you think along those lines, the idea of God being the giver of gifts isn't too far-fetched. And it goes beyond these so called costly items of life. If you count the small things; you are surrounded by presents not just every day but probably every moment. When you take note of every moment of happiness placed in your life, you'll see that you unwittingly unwrap hundreds of gifts throughout your day and not just on those special occasions.

And that is what King Solomon understood when he rejoiced in the little things. He sure had a vast kingdom with more things than anyone could ever enjoy in two lifetimes; yet, he was quick to note that it was all "vanity" (Ecclesiastes 1:2).

Part of the fall of man is a tendency to focus on the negative, and let's be real, there's plenty of that happening around. One bad minute can ruin your whole day. But what would it look like if we stay focused on all the good and see how it outweighs the bad? Just the little things! Because everything is a gift from God, and knowing that He loves us so much leads us to nothing less than gratitude and deep devotion.

One of God's hearts' desires is to never stop surprising us with amazing gifts. James 1:17 says, *"Every good gift and every perfect gift is from above, coming down from the Father of lights with whom there is no variation or shadow due to change."* Every good gift you receive is because God loves you immensely. His love for you is so great that He looks for every opportunity to give you a gift. He desperately wants you to know that you are so much loved and valued by Him and that He is not distant from you but, rather, is working in your midst to lead you to abundant joy, peace and life.

Matthew 7:11 says, *"If you then, who are evil, know how to give good gifts to your children, how much more will your Father who is in heaven give good things to those who ask him!"* I love how God has chosen to be known to us as a Father. God longs to bless you the way a good Father would, while yet loving you more deeply and powerfully than any earthly parent ever could, by outdoing any example an earthly father gives us. What gift are you longing for today? God's gifts may not look like a present you opened for Christmas last year, or the one you received for your birthday, but they will be exactly what you need when you need it. God so longs for you to know the depth of His love that He sent His only begotten Son to die for you! Ask the Spirit to give you eyes to see all the ways He is working in your life. Whatever gift you need from God today, His word promises in 1 John 5:15, *"if we know that He hears us in whatever we ask, we know that we have the requests that we have asked of Him."* Our Daddy God hears you today. And what's more, He will respond to you perfectly-the right time, the right way, as only He knows what you need and when you need it. Just trust and thank Him.

As we've seen, God's gifts are much more life-giving than anything an earthly parent could give. He provides whatever you need because He cares about everything you need and desires to use you to bless others. We are to share the 'gifts' God has given us, to uplift and inspire and challenge each other. Our gifts are meant for encouraging others to rise to their full potential in God. We are all here on this earth- each like a piece of puzzle, each one complimenting and supplementing each other. We all have been given a gift that we can use to help someone else along the way. No matter what it is – big or small – we have a part to play and we can use our gifts eventually for God's glory.

If you aret not sure what 'gift' or 'talent' you may have that God has given you – ask Him to reveal it to you. It may be what you consider a 'natural ability' or 'talent', but when it's dedicated to the Lord, He can use it for His purposes. After all, even our natural abilities and talents are a gift from God. He has given it to us so we can use it to encourage and inspire others, and therefore glorify God.

Spend some time today reflecting on the amazing gifts He has given you. Thank Him for His desire to bless you, while opening your heart to receive all the gifts your heavenly Father longs to give you today.

# 31 Days on how to
# F.E.A.S.T. and
# Enjoy the 5G Network of GOD!

# Day-1

## Goodness

**Genesis 1.31**: *And God saw everything that He had made, and behold, it was very good.*

## Greatness

**1 Chronicles 16.25:** *For great is the LORD, and greatly to be praised; He also is to be feared above all gods.*

## Glory

**Exodus 24.15, 16:** *Then Moses went up into the mountain, and a cloud covered the mountain. Now the glory of the Lord rested on Mount Sinai, and the cloud covered it six days. And on the seventh day, He called to Moses, out of the midst of the cloud.*

## Grace

**Hebrews 4.16**: *Let us then with confidence draw near to the throne of grace, that we may receive mercy and find grace to help in time of need.*

## Gifts

**Psalm 84:11**: *For the Lord God is a sun and shield; the Lord bestows favor and honor. No good thing does He withhold from those who walk uprightly.*

**Now how do you F.E.A.S.T. and Enjoy the 5G Network of GOD?**

F- **Focus**: Ask the Holy Spirit to help you focus your mind and heart on HIM alone, removing every distraction. (List your distractions that are preventing you from focusing on HIM)

_______________________________________________

_______________________________________________

_______________________________________________

**E- Examine** the 5 verses above: Meditate on them. What stands out from these verses to you?

What do you feel God is telling you in these verses? What do they mean to you? Where all have you seen or experienced HIS 5G's today?

_______________________________________________

_______________________________________________

_______________________________________________

_______________________________________________

**A- Assess** and apply it: Ask the Holy Spirit to give you a deeper revelation of these 5G's. Any attributes of God that strikes you. What does this revelation of HIM do to you? How will you follow through?

_______________________________________________

_______________________________________________

_______________________________________________

_______________________________________________

**S- Share it.** With every opportunity you get today, tell others. Boast about our God! List who can you tell and what will you tell them.

_______________________________________________

_______________________________________________

_______________________________________________

_______________________________________________

**T- Thank** and Praise Him for what He has shown you in these verses or around today. Set your mind and heart in an attitude of worship now!

_______________________________________________

_______________________________________________

_______________________________________________

# Day-2

## Goodness

**Exodus 33.19**: *And He said, "I will make all my goodness pass before you and will proclaim before you My Name 'The Lord.' And I will be gracious to whom I will be gracious, and will show mercy on whom I will show mercy.*

## Greatness

**1 Chronicles 29:11**: *Yours, O LORD, is the greatness and the power and the glory and the victory and the majesty, indeed everything that is in the heavens and the earth; Yours is the dominion, O LORD, and You exalt Yourself as head over all.*

## Glory

**Exodus 33.18, 19**: *And he said, "Pl show me Your Glory" And He said, "I will make all My goodness pass before you, and I will proclaim the name of the Lord before you."*

## Grace

**Ephesians 2.8**: *For by grace you have been saved through faith. And this is not your own doing; it is the gift of God.*

## Gifts

**Psalm 127:3**: *Behold, children are a heritage from the Lord, the fruit of the womb a reward.*

## Now how do you F.E.A.S.T. and Enjoy the 5G Network of GOD?

**F- Focus**: Ask the Holy Spirit to help you focus your mind and heart on HIM alone, removing every distraction. (List your distractions that are preventing you from focusing on HIM)

______________________________________________

______________________________________________

______________________________________________

______________________________________________

**E- Examine** the 5 verses above: Meditate on them. What stands out from these verses to you?

What do you feel God is telling you in these verses? What do they mean to you? Where all have you seen or experienced HIS 5G's today?

_______________________________________________

_______________________________________________

_______________________________________________

_______________________________________________

**A- Assess** and apply it: Ask the Holy Spirit to give you a deeper revelation of these 5G's. Any attributes of God that strikes you. What does this revelation of HIM do to you? How will you follow through?

_______________________________________________

_______________________________________________

_______________________________________________

_______________________________________________

**S- Share it**. With every opportunity you get today, tell others. Boast about our God! List who can you tell and what will you tell them.

_______________________________________________

_______________________________________________

_______________________________________________

_______________________________________________

**T- Thank** and Praise Him for what He has shown you in these verses or around today. Set your mind and heart in an attitude of worship now!

_______________________________________________

_______________________________________________

_______________________________________________

# Day-3

## Goodness

**1 Chronicles 16.34**: *Oh give thanks to the Lord, for He is good; for His steadfast love endures forever!*

## Greatness

**Jeremiah 10:6:** *There is none like You, O LORD; You are great, and great is Your name in might*

## Glory

**Exodus 40.34, 35:** *Then the cloud covered the tabernacle of meeting, and the glory of the Lord filled the tabernacle. And Moses was not able to enter the tabernacle of meeting, because the cloud rested above it, and the glory of the Lord filled the tabernacle.*

## Grace

**James 4.6**: *But He gives more grace. Therefore it says, "God opposes the proud, but gives grace to the humble."*

## Gifts

**Ecclesiastes 3:13**: *Also that everyone should eat and drink and take pleasure in all his toil—this is God's gift to man.*

## Now how do you F.E.A.S.T. and Enjoy the 5G Network of GOD?

**F- Focus**: Ask the Holy Spirit to help you focus your mind and heart on HIM alone, removing every distraction. (List your distractions that are preventing you from focusing on HIM)

______________________________________________

______________________________________________

______________________________________________

______________________________________________

**E- Examine** the 5 verses above: Meditate on them. What stands out from these verses to you?

What do you feel God is telling you in these verses? What do they mean to you? Where all have you seen or experienced HIS 5G's today?

_______________________________________________

_______________________________________________

_______________________________________________

_______________________________________________

**A- Assess** and apply it: Ask the Holy Spirit to give you a deeper revelation of these 5G's. Any attributes of God that strikes you. What does this revelation of HIM do to you? How will you follow through?

_______________________________________________

_______________________________________________

_______________________________________________

_______________________________________________

**S- Share it**. With every opportunity you get today, tell others. Boast about our God! List who can you tell and what will you tell them.

_______________________________________________

_______________________________________________

_______________________________________________

_______________________________________________

**T- Thank** and Praise Him for what He has shown you in these verses or around today. Set your mind and heart in an attitude of worship now!

_______________________________________________

_______________________________________________

_______________________________________________

_______________________________________________

# Day-4

## Goodness

**Ezra 3.11**: *And they sang responsively, praising and giving thanks to the Lord: "For He is good, for His mercy endures forever toward Israel."*

## Greatness

**Nehemiah 1:5**: *I said, "I beseech You, O LORD God of heaven, the great and awesome God, who preserves the covenant and lovingkindness for those who love Him and keep His commandments"*

## Glory

**Numbers 14.21**: *But truly, as I live, all the earth shall be filled with the GLORY of the Lord.*

## Grace

**Romans 11.6**: *But if it is by grace, it is no longer on the basis of works; otherwise grace would no longer be grace.*

## Gifts

**Ecclesiastes 5:19**: *Everyone also to whom God has given wealth and possessions and power to enjoy them, and to accept his lot and rejoice in his toil—this is the gift of God.*

### Now how do you F.E.A.S.T. and Enjoy the 5G Network of GOD?

**F- Focus**: Ask the Holy Spirit to help you focus your mind and heart on HIM alone, removing every distraction. (List your distractions that are preventing you from focusing on HIM)

__________________________________________________

__________________________________________________

__________________________________________________

__________________________________________________

**E- Examine** the 5 verses above: Meditate on them. What stands out from these verses to you?

What do you feel God is telling you in these verses? What do they mean to you? Where all have you seen or experienced HIS 5G's today?

__________________________________________________

__________________________________________________

__________________________________________________

__________________________________________________

**A- Assess** and apply it: Ask the Holy Spirit to give you a deeper revelation of these 5G's. Any attributes of God that strikes you. What does this revelation of HIM do to you? How will you follow through?

__________________________________________________

__________________________________________________

__________________________________________________

__________________________________________________

**S- Share it**. With every opportunity you get today, tell others. Boast about our God! List who can you tell and what will you tell them.

__________________________________________________

__________________________________________________

__________________________________________________

__________________________________________________

**T- Thank** and Praise Him for what He has shown you in these verses or around today. Set your mind and heart in an attitude of worship now!

__________________________________________________

__________________________________________________

__________________________________________________

__________________________________________________

# Day-5

## Goodness

**Nehemiah 9.20**: *You also gave Your good Spirit to instruct them, and did not withhold Your manna from their mouth, and gave them water for their thirst.*

## Greatness

**Ezekiel 36.23:** *I will vindicate the holiness of My great name which has been profaned among the nations, which you have profaned in their midst Then the nations will know that I am the LORD," declares the Lord GOD, "when I prove Myself holy among you in their sight.*

## Glory

**Deuteronomy 5.24:** *And you said: "Surely the Lord our God has shown us His glory and greatness, and we have heard His voice from the midst of the fire."*

## Grace

**Titus 2.11**: *For the grace of God has appeared, bringing salvation for all people.*

## Gifts

**Matthew 7:7**: *Ask, and it will be given to you; seek, and you will find; knock, and it will be opened to you.*

## Now how do you F.E.A.S.T. and Enjoy the 5G Network of GOD?

F- Focus: Ask the Holy Spirit to help you focus your mind and heart on HIM alone, removing every distraction. (List your distractions that are preventing you from focusing on HIM)

_________________________________________________

_________________________________________________

_________________________________________________

_________________________________________________

**E- Examine** the 5 verses above: Meditate on them. What stands out from these verses to you?

What do you feel God is telling you in these verses? What do they mean to you? Where all have you seen or experienced HIS 5G's today?

_______________________________________________

_______________________________________________

_______________________________________________

_______________________________________________

**A- Assess** and apply it: Ask the Holy Spirit to give you a deeper revelation of these 5G's. Any attributes of God that strikes you. What does this revelation of HIM do to you? How will you follow through?

_______________________________________________

_______________________________________________

_______________________________________________

_______________________________________________

**S- Share it**. With every opportunity you get today, tell others. Boast about our God! List who can you tell and what will you tell them.

_______________________________________________

_______________________________________________

_______________________________________________

_______________________________________________

**T- Thank** and Praise Him for what He has shown you in these verses or around today. Set your mind and heart in an attitude of worship now!

_______________________________________________

_______________________________________________

_______________________________________________

_______________________________________________

# Day-6

## Goodness
**Psalm 16.2**: *Every good thing I have comes from You.*

## Greatness
**1 Samuel 12.22:** *For the LORD will not abandon His people on account of His great name, because the LORD has been pleased to make you a people for Himself.*

## Glory
**1 Kings 8.10, 11:** *And it came to pass, when the priests came out of the holy place that the cloud filled the house of the Lord, so that the priests could not continue ministering because of the cloud; for the GLORY of the Lord filled the house of the Lord.*

## Grace
**1 Corinthians 15.10**: *But by the grace of God I am what I am, and His grace toward me was not in vain. On the contrary, I worked harder than any of them, though it was not I, but the grace of God that is with me.*

## Gifts
**Matthew 7:11:** *If you then, who are evil, know how to give good gifts to your children, how much more will your Father who is in heaven give good things to those who ask him!*

### Now how do you F.E.A.S.T. and Enjoy the 5G Network of GOD?

**F- Focus**: Ask the Holy Spirit to help you focus your mind and heart on HIM alone, removing every distraction. (List your distractions that are preventing you from focusing on HIM)

_______________________________________________

_______________________________________________

_______________________________________________

_______________________________________________

**E- Examine** the 5 verses above: Meditate on them. What stands out from these verses to you?

What do you feel God is telling you in these verses? What do they mean to you? Where all have you seen or experienced HIS 5G's today?

_______________________________________________

_______________________________________________

_______________________________________________

_______________________________________________

**A- Assess** and apply it: Ask the Holy Spirit to give you a deeper revelation of these 5G's. Any attributes of God that strikes you. What does this revelation of HIM do to you? How will you follow through?

_______________________________________________

_______________________________________________

_______________________________________________

_______________________________________________

**S- Share it**. With every opportunity you get today, tell others. Boast about our God! List who can you tell and what will you tell them.

_______________________________________________

_______________________________________________

_______________________________________________

_______________________________________________

**T- Thank** and Praise Him for what He has shown you in these verses or around today. Set your mind and heart in an attitude of worship now!

_______________________________________________

_______________________________________________

_______________________________________________

# Day-7

## Goodness

**Psalm 23.6:** *Surely goodness and mercy shall follow me all the days of my life, and I shall dwell in the house of the Lord forever.*

## Greatness

**1 Kings 8.42:** *(...for they will hear of Your great name and Your mighty hand, and of Your outstretched arm); when he comes and prays toward this house,*

## Glory

**1 Chronicles 29.11:** *Yours, O Lord, is the greatness, the power and the GLORY, the victory and the majesty; for all that is in heaven and in earth is Yours; Yours is the kingdom, O Lord, and You are exalted as head over all.*

## Grace

**1 Peter 4.10**: *As each has received a gift, use it to serve one another, as good stewards of God's varied grace.*

## Gifts

**Matthew 25:15**: *To one he gave five talents, to another two, to another one, to each according to his ability. Then he went away.*

**Now how do you F.E.A.S.T. and Enjoy the 5G Network of GOD?**

**F- Focus**: Ask the Holy Spirit to help you focus your mind and heart on HIM alone, removing every distraction. (List your distractions that are preventing you from focusing on HIM)

_______________________________________________

_______________________________________________

_______________________________________________

_______________________________________________

**E- Examine** the 5 verses above: Meditate on them. What stands out from these verses to you?

What do you feel God is telling you in these verses? What do they mean to you? Where all have you seen or experienced HIS 5G's today?

___________________________________________

___________________________________________

___________________________________________

___________________________________________

**A- Assess** and apply it: Ask the Holy Spirit to give you a deeper revelation of these 5G's. Any attributes of God that strikes you. What does this revelation of HIM do to you? How will you follow through?

___________________________________________

___________________________________________

___________________________________________

___________________________________________

**S- Share it.** With every opportunity you get today, tell others. Boast about our God! List who can you tell and what will you tell them.

___________________________________________

___________________________________________

___________________________________________

**T- Thank** and Praise Him for what He has shown you in these verses or around today. Set your mind and heart in an attitude of worship now!

___________________________________________

___________________________________________

___________________________________________

# Day-8

## Goodness

**Psalm 25.7**: *Remember not the sins of my youth or my transgressions; according to Your steadfast love remember me, for the sake of Your goodness, O Lord!*

## Greatness

**Psalm 47.2:** *For the LORD Most High is to be feared, A great King over all the earth".*

## Glory

**2 Chronicles 7.1-3:** *When Solomon had finished praying, fire came down from heaven and consumed the burnt offerings and sacrifices: and the GLORY of the Lord filled the temple. And the priests could not enter the house of the Lord, because the GLORY of the Lord had filled the Lord's house. When all the children of Israel saw how the fire came down, and the GLORY of the Lord on the temple, they bowed their faces to the ground on the pavement, and worshipped and praised the Lord...*

## Grace

**1 Peter 5.10**: *And after you have suffered a little while, the God of all grace, who has called you to His eternal glory in Christ, will Himself restore, confirm, strengthen, and establish you.*

## Gifts

**Luke 12:32**: *Fear not, little flock, for it is your Father's good pleasure to give you the kingdom.*

## Now how do you F.E.A.S.T. and Enjoy the 5G Network of GOD?

**F- Focus**: Ask the Holy Spirit to help you focus your mind and heart on HIM alone, removing every distraction. (List your distractions that are preventing you from focusing on HIM)

_______________________________________________________

_______________________________________________________

___________________________________________

___________________________________________

**E- Examine** the 5 verses above: Meditate on them. What stands out from these verses to you?

What do you feel God is telling you in these verses? What do they mean to you? Where all have you seen or experienced HIS 5G's today?

___________________________________________

___________________________________________

___________________________________________

**A- Assess** and apply it: Ask the Holy Spirit to give you a deeper revelation of these 5G's. Any attributes of God that strikes you. What does this revelation of HIM do to you? How will you follow through?

___________________________________________

___________________________________________

___________________________________________

___________________________________________

**S- Share it**. With every opportunity you get today, tell others. Boast about our God! List who can you tell and what will you tell them.

___________________________________________

___________________________________________

___________________________________________

**T- Thank** and Praise Him for what He has shown you in these verses or around today. Set your mind and heart in an attitude of worship now!

___________________________________________

___________________________________________

___________________________________________

___________________________________________

# Day-9

### Goodness

**Psalm 27.13**: *I believe that I shall look upon the goodness of the Lord in the land of the living!*

### Greatness

**Psalm 104.1:** *Bless the LORD, O my soul! O LORD my God, You are very great; You are clothed with splendor and majesty*

### Glory

**Psalms 8.1:** *O Lord, our Lord, how excellent is Your name in all the earth, Who have set Your GLORY above the heavens!*

### Grace

**2 Corinthians 12.9**: *But He said to me, "My grace is sufficient for you, for My power is made perfect in weakness." Therefore I will boast all the more gladly of my weaknesses, so that the power of Christ may rest upon me.*

### Gifts

**John 3:16:** *For God so loved the world, that He gave His only begotten Son, that whosoever believeth in Him should not perish, but have everlasting life.*

## Now how do you F.E.A.S.T. and Enjoy the 5G Network of GOD?

**F- Focus**: Ask the Holy Spirit to help you focus your mind and heart on HIM alone, removing every distraction. (List your distractions that are preventing you from focusing on HIM)

_______________________________________________

_______________________________________________

_______________________________________________

_______________________________________________

**E- Examine** the 5 verses above: Meditate on them. What stands out from these verses to you?

What do you feel God is telling you in these verses? What do they mean to you? Where all have you seen or experienced HIS 5G's today?

___________________________________________

___________________________________________

___________________________________________

___________________________________________

**A- Assess** and apply it: Ask the Holy Spirit to give you a deeper revelation of these 5G's. Any attributes of God that strikes you. What does this revelation of HIM do to you? How will you follow through?

___________________________________________

___________________________________________

___________________________________________

___________________________________________

**S- Share it**. With every opportunity you get today, tell others. Boast about our God! List who can you tell and what will you tell them.

___________________________________________

___________________________________________

___________________________________________

___________________________________________

**T- Thank** and Praise Him for what He has shown you in these verses or around today. Set your mind and heart in an attitude of worship now!

___________________________________________

___________________________________________

___________________________________________

___________________________________________

# Day-10

## Goodness

**Psalm 31.19:** *Oh, how abundant is your goodness, which you have stored up for those who fear You and worked for those who take refuge in You, in the sight of the children of mankind!*

## Greatness

**Malachi 1.11:** *For from the rising of the sun to its setting My Name will be great among the nations, and in every place incense will be offered to My Name, and a pure offering. For My Name will be great among the nations, says the Lord of hosts.*

## Glory

**Psalms 19.1:** *The heavens declare the GLORY of God; and the firmament shows His handiwork.*

## Grace

**2 Corinthians 8.9**: For *you know the grace of our Lord Jesus Christ, that though He was rich, yet for your sake He became poor, so that you by His poverty might become rich.*

## Gifts

**John 4:10**: *Jesus answered her, "If you knew the gift of God, and who it is that is saying to you, 'Give me a drink,' you would have asked Him, and He would have given you living water."*

**Now how do you F.E.A.S.T. and Enjoy the 5G Network of GOD?F- Focus**: Ask the Holy Spirit to help you focus your mind and heart on HIM alone, removing every distraction. (List your distractions that are preventing you from focusing on HIM)

_______________________________________________

_______________________________________________

_______________________________________________

**E- Examine** the 5 verses above: Meditate on them. What stands out from these verses to you?

What do you feel God is telling you in these verses? What do they mean to you? Where all have you seen or experienced HIS 5G's today?

_______________________________________________

_______________________________________________

_______________________________________________

_______________________________________________

**A- Assess** and apply it: Ask the Holy Spirit to give you a deeper revelation of these 5G's. Any attributes of God that strikes you. What does this revelation of HIM do to you? How will you follow through?

_______________________________________________

_______________________________________________

_______________________________________________

_______________________________________________

**S- Share it**. With every opportunity you get today, tell others. Boast about our God! List who can you tell and what will you tell them.

_______________________________________________

_______________________________________________

_______________________________________________

_______________________________________________

**T- Thank** and Praise Him for what He has shown you in these verses or around today. Set your mind and heart in an attitude of worship now!

_______________________________________________

_______________________________________________

_______________________________________________

_______________________________________________

# Day-11

## Goodness
**Psalm 34.8**: *Oh, taste and see that the Lord is good! Blessed is the man who takes refuge in Him!*

## Greatness
**Psalms 135.5**: *For I know that the Lord is great, and that our Lord is above all gods.*

## Glory
**Psalms 24.7, 8**: *Lift up your heads, O you gates! And be lifted up, you everlasting doors! And the King of GLORY shall come in. Who is this King of GLORY? The Lord strong and mighty, the Lord mighty in battle.*

## Grace
**2 Corinthians 9.8**: *And God is able to make all grace abound to you, so that having all sufficiency in all things at all times, you may abound in every good work.*

## Gifts
**Acts 2:38**: *And Peter said to them, "Repent and be baptized every one of you in the name of Jesus Christ for the forgiveness of your sins, and you will receive the gift of the Holy Spirit".*

**Now how do you F.E.A.S.T. and Enjoy the 5G Network of GOD?**

F- Focus: Ask the Holy Spirit to help you focus your mind and heart on HIM alone, removing every distraction. (List your distractions that are preventing you from focusing on HIM)

_______________________________________________

_______________________________________________

_______________________________________________

**E- Examine** the 5 verses above: Meditate on them. What stands out from these verses to you?

What do you feel God is telling you in these verses? What do they mean to you? Where all have you seen or experienced HIS 5G's today?

_______________________________________________

_______________________________________________

_______________________________________________

_______________________________________________

**A- Assess** and apply it: Ask the Holy Spirit to give you a deeper revelation of these 5G's. Any attributes of God that strikes you. What does this revelation of HIM do to you? How will you follow through?

_______________________________________________

_______________________________________________

_______________________________________________

_______________________________________________

**S- Share it**. With every opportunity you get today, tell others. Boast about our God! List who can you tell and what will you tell them.

_______________________________________________

_______________________________________________

_______________________________________________

**T- Thank** and Praise Him for what He has shown you in these verses or around today. Set your mind and heart in an attitude of worship now!

_______________________________________________

_______________________________________________

_______________________________________________

_______________________________________________

# Day-12

## Goodness

**Psalm 65.4**: *Blessed is the one You choose and bring near, to dwell in Your courts! We shall be satisfied with the goodness of Your house, the holiness of Your temple!*

## Greatness

**Psalm 136.4:** *To Him who alone does great wonders, For His lovingkindness is everlasting;*

## Glory

**Psalm 29.3:** *The voice of the LORD is over the waters; the GOD of GLORY thunders; the LORD is over many waters.*

## Grace

**2 Peter 1.2**: *May grace and peace be multiplied to you in the knowledge of God and of Jesus our Lord.*

## Gifts

**Romans 5:17**: *For if, because of one man's trespass, death reigned through that one man, much more will those who receive the abundance of grace and the free gift of righteousness reign in life through the one man Jesus Christ.*

## Now how do you F.E.A.S.T. and Enjoy the 5G Network of GOD?

**F- Focus**: Ask the Holy Spirit to help you focus your mind and heart on HIM alone, removing every distraction. (List your distractions that are preventing you from focusing on HIM)

___________________________________________
___________________________________________
___________________________________________
___________________________________________

**E- Examine** the 5 verses above: Meditate on them. What stands out from these verses to you?

What do you feel God is telling you in these verses? What do they mean to you? Where all have you seen or experienced HIS 5G's today?

_______________________________________________

_______________________________________________

_______________________________________________

_______________________________________________

**A- Assess** and apply it: Ask the Holy Spirit to give you a deeper revelation of these 5G's. Any attributes of God that strikes you. What does this revelation of HIM do to you? How will you follow through?

_______________________________________________

_______________________________________________

_______________________________________________

_______________________________________________

**S- Share it**. With every opportunity you get today, tell others. Boast about our God! List who can you tell and what will you tell them.

_______________________________________________

_______________________________________________

_______________________________________________

_______________________________________________

**T- Thank** and Praise Him for what He has shown you in these verses or around today. Set your mind and heart in an attitude of worship now!

_______________________________________________

_______________________________________________

_______________________________________________

_______________________________________________

# Day-13

## Goodness
**Psalm 65.11:** *You crown the year with Your goodness, and Your paths drip with abundance.*

## Greatness
**Deuteronomy 10:17:** *For the Lord your God is God of gods and Lord of lords, the great, the mighty, and the awesome God, who is not partial and takes no bribe*

## Glory
**Psalms 57.5:** *Be exalted, O God, above the havens; let Your GLORY be above all the earth.*

## Grace
**2 Timothy 1.9:** *Who saved us and called us to a holy calling, not because of our works but because of His own purpose and grace, which He gave us in Christ Jesus before the ages began.*

## Gifts
**Romans 6:23:** *For the wages of sin is death, but the free gift of God is eternal life in Christ Jesus our Lord.*

**Now how do you F.E.A.S.T. and Enjoy the 5G Network of GOD?**

**F- Focus**: Ask the Holy Spirit to help you focus your mind and heart on HIM alone, removing every distraction. (List your distractions that are preventing you from focusing on HIM)

______________________________________

______________________________________

______________________________________

______________________________________

**E- Examine** the 5 verses above: Meditate on them. What stands out from these verses to you?

What do you feel God is telling you in these verses? What do they mean to you? Where all have you seen or experienced HIS 5G's today?

_______________________________________________

_______________________________________________

_______________________________________________

_______________________________________________

**A- Assess** and apply it: Ask the Holy Spirit to give you a deeper revelation of these 5G's. Any attributes of God that strikes you. What does this revelation of HIM do to you? How will you follow through?

_______________________________________________

_______________________________________________

_______________________________________________

_______________________________________________

**S- Share it**. With every opportunity you get today, tell others. Boast about our God! List who can you tell and what will you tell them.

_______________________________________________

_______________________________________________

_______________________________________________

_______________________________________________

**T- Thank** and Praise Him for what He has shown you in these verses or around today. Set your mind and heart in an attitude of worship now!

_______________________________________________

_______________________________________________

_______________________________________________

_______________________________________________

# Day-14

## Goodness

**Psalm 84.11**: *For the Lord God is a sun and shield; the Lord bestows favor and honor. No good thing does He withhold from those who walk uprightly.*

## Greatness

**Jeremiah 32:19:** *...great in counsel and mighty indeed, Whose eyes are open to all the ways of the sons of men, giving to everyone according to his ways and according to the fruit of his deeds;*

## Glory

**Psalm 63.2:** *So I have looked for you in the sanctuary, to see Your power and Your GLORY.*

## Grace

**2 Timothy 2.1**: *You then, my child, be strengthened by the grace that is in Christ Jesus.*

## Gifts

**Romans 11:29:** *For the gifts and the calling of God are irrevocable.*

## Now how do you F.E.A.S.T. and Enjoy the 5G Network of GOD?

**F- Focus**: Ask the Holy Spirit to help you focus your mind and heart on HIM alone, removing every distraction. (List your distractions that are preventing you from focusing on HIM)

___________________________________________

___________________________________________

___________________________________________

___________________________________________

**E- Examine** the 5 verses above: Meditate on them. What stands out from these verses to you?

What do you feel God is telling you in these verses? What do they mean to you? Where all have you seen or experienced HIS 5G's today?

______________________________________________

______________________________________________

______________________________________________

______________________________________________

**A- Assess** and apply it: Ask the Holy Spirit to give you a deeper revelation of these 5G's. Any attributes of God that strikes you. What does this revelation of HIM do to you? How will you follow through?

______________________________________________

______________________________________________

______________________________________________

______________________________________________

**S- Share it**. With every opportunity you get today, tell others. Boast about our God! List who can you tell and what will you tell them.

______________________________________________

______________________________________________

______________________________________________

______________________________________________

**T- Thank** and Praise Him for what He has shown you in these verses or around today. Set your mind and heart in an attitude of worship now!

______________________________________________

______________________________________________

______________________________________________

# Day-15

## Goodness

**Psalm 86.5**: *For You, O Lord, are good and forgiving, abounding in steadfast love to all who call upon You.*

## Greatness

**Luke 1:49:** *For the Mighty One has done great things for me; And holy is His name.*

## Glory

**Psalm 72.19:** *Blessed be His glorious name forever! And let the whole earth be filled with His GLORY. Amen and Amen.*

## Grace

**Acts 15.11**: *But we believe that we will be saved through the grace of the Lord Jesus, just as they will."*

## Gifts

**1 Corinthians 12:4-6**: *Now there are varieties of gifts, but the same Spirit; and there are varieties of service, but the same Lord; and there are varieties of activities, but it is the same God who empowers them all in everyone.*

### Now how do you F.E.A.S.T. and Enjoy the 5G Network of GOD?

**F- Focus**: Ask the Holy Spirit to help you focus your mind and heart on HIM alone, removing every distraction. (List your distractions that are preventing you from focusing on HIM)

______________________________________________

______________________________________________

______________________________________________

______________________________________________

**E- Examine** the 5 verses above: Meditate on them. What stands out from these verses to you?

What do you feel God is telling you in these verses? What do they mean to you? Where all have you seen or experienced HIS 5G's today?

_______________________________________________

_______________________________________________

_______________________________________________

_______________________________________________

**A- Assess** and apply it: Ask the Holy Spirit to give you a deeper revelation of these 5G's. Any attributes of God that strikes you. What does this revelation of HIM do to you? How will you follow through?

_______________________________________________

_______________________________________________

_______________________________________________

_______________________________________________

**S- Share it**. With every opportunity you get today, tell others. Boast about our God! List who can you tell and what will you tell them.

_______________________________________________

_______________________________________________

_______________________________________________

_______________________________________________

**T- Thank** and Praise Him for what He has shown you in these verses or around today. Set your mind and heart in an attitude of worship now!

_______________________________________________

_______________________________________________

_______________________________________________

_______________________________________________

# Day-16

## Goodness

**Psalm 107.8-9:** *Oh, that men would give thanks to the Lord for His goodness, and for His wonderful works to the children of men! For He satisfies the longing soul, and fills the hungry soul with goodness.*

## Greatness

**Deuteronomy 9.29:** *Yet they are Your people, even Your inheritance, whom You have brought out by Your great power and Your outstretched arm*

## Glory

**Psalm 102.16:** *The Lord shall build up Zion; He shall appear in His GLORY.*

## Grace

**Acts 20.32:** *And now I commend you to God and to the word of His grace, which is able to build you up and to give you the inheritance among all those who are sanctified.*

## Gifts

**1 Corinthians 12:7-11:** *To each is given the manifestation of the Spirit for the common good. For to one is given through the Spirit the utterance of wisdom, and to another the utterance of knowledge according to the same Spirit, to another faith by the same Spirit, to another gifts of healing by the one Spirit, to another the working of miracles, to another prophecy, to another the ability to distinguish between spirits, to another various kinds of tongues, to another the interpretation of tongues. All these are empowered by one and the same Spirit, Who apportions to each one individually as He wills.*

### Now how do you F.E.A.S.T. and Enjoy the 5G Network of GOD?

**F- Focus**: Ask the Holy Spirit to help you focus your mind and heart on HIM alone, removing every distraction. (List your distractions that are preventing you from focusing on HIM)

_______________________________________

_______________________________________

_______________________________________

_______________________________________

**E- Examine** the 5 verses above: Meditate on them. What stands out from these verses to you?

What do you feel God is telling you in these verses? What do they mean to you? Where all have you seen or experienced HIS 5G's today?

_______________________________________

_______________________________________

_______________________________________

_______________________________________

**A- Assess** and apply it: Ask the Holy Spirit to give you a deeper revelation of these 5G's. Any attributes of God that strikes you. What does this revelation of HIM do to you? How will you follow through?

_______________________________________

_______________________________________

_______________________________________

_______________________________________

**S- Share it**. With every opportunity you get today, tell others. Boast about our God! List who can you tell and what will you tell them.

_______________________________________

_______________________________________

_______________________________________

**T- Thank** and Praise Him for what He has shown you in these verses or around today. Set your mind and heart in an attitude of worship now!

_______________________________________

_______________________________________

_______________________________________

_______________________________________

# Day-17

## Goodness
**Psalm 119.68**: *You are good and do good; teach me Your statutes.*

## Greatness
**Exodus 15.7:** *And in the greatness of Your excellence You overthrow those who rise up against You; You send forth Your burning anger, and it consumes them as chaff.*

## Glory
**Psalms 104.31**: *May the GLORY of the Lord endure forever; may the Lord rejoice in His works.*

## Grace
**Acts 4.33**: *And with great power the apostles were giving their testimony to the resurrection of the Lord Jesus, and great grace was upon them all.*

## Gifts
**1 Corinthians 14:1**: *Pursue love, and earnestly desire the spiritual gifts, especially that you may prophesy.*

## Now how do you F.E.A.S.T. and Enjoy the 5G Network of GOD?

F- **Focus**: Ask the Holy Spirit to help you focus your mind and heart on HIM alone, removing every distraction. (List your distractions that are preventing you from focusing on HIM)

______________________________________________

______________________________________________

______________________________________________

______________________________________________

**E- Examine** the 5 verses above: Meditate on them. What stands out from these verses to you?

What do you feel God is telling you in these verses? What do they mean to you? Where all have you seen or experienced HIS 5G's today?

___________________________________________

___________________________________________

___________________________________________

___________________________________________

**A- Assess** and apply it: Ask the Holy Spirit to give you a deeper revelation of these 5G's. Any attributes of God that strikes you. What does this revelation of HIM do to you? How will you follow through?

___________________________________________

___________________________________________

___________________________________________

___________________________________________

**S- Share it**. With every opportunity you get today, tell others. Boast about our God! List who can you tell and what will you tell them.

___________________________________________

___________________________________________

___________________________________________

___________________________________________

**T- Thank** and Praise Him for what He has shown you in these verses or around today. Set your mind and heart in an attitude of worship now!

___________________________________________

___________________________________________

___________________________________________

___________________________________________

# Day-18

### Goodness

**Psalm 135.3**: *Praise the Lord, for the Lord is good; sing to His name, for it is pleasant!*

### Greatness

**Deuteronomy 9:26**: *I prayed to the LORD and said, 'O Lord GOD, do not destroy Your people, even Your inheritance, whom You have redeemed through Your greatness, whom You have brought out of Egypt with a mighty hand.*

### Glory

**Psalms 113.4**: *The Lord is high above all nations, His GLORY above the heavens.*

### Grace

**Ephesians 1.6**: *To the praise of His glorious grace, with which He has blessed us in the Beloved.*

### Gifts

**2 Corinthians 9:10**: *He who supplies seed to the sower and bread for food will supply and multiply your seed for sowing and increase the harvest of your righteousness.*

### Now how do you F.E.A.S.T. and Enjoy the 5G Network of GOD?

**F- Focus**: Ask the Holy Spirit to help you focus your mind and heart on HIM alone, removing every distraction. (List your distractions that are preventing you from focusing on HIM)

_________________________________________________
_________________________________________________
_________________________________________________
_________________________________________________

**E- Examine** the 5 verses above: Meditate on them. What stands out from these verses to you?

What do you feel God is telling you in these verses? What do they mean to you? Where all have you seen or experienced HIS 5G's today?

_______________________________________________

_______________________________________________

_______________________________________________

_______________________________________________

**A- Assess** and apply it: Ask the Holy Spirit to give you a deeper revelation of these 5G's. Any attributes of God that strikes you. What does this revelation of HIM do to you? How will you follow through?

_______________________________________________

_______________________________________________

_______________________________________________

_______________________________________________

**S- Share it**. With every opportunity you get today, tell others. Boast about our God! List who can you tell and what will you tell them.

_______________________________________________

_______________________________________________

_______________________________________________

_______________________________________________

**T- Thank** and Praise Him for what He has shown you in these verses or around today. Set your mind and heart in an attitude of worship now!

_______________________________________________

_______________________________________________

_______________________________________________

# Day-19

## Goodness

**Psalm 145.5-7**: *I will meditate on the glorious splendor of Your majesty, and on Your wondrous works. Men shall speak of the might of Your awesome acts, and I will declare Your greatness. They shall utter the memory of Your great goodness, and shall sing of Your righteousness.*

## Greatness

**Isaiah 40.26**: *Lift up your eyes on high and see who has created these stars, The One who leads forth their host by number, He calls them all by name; Because of the greatness of His might and the strength of His power, Not one of them is missing.*

## Glory

**Psalms 138.5:** *Yes, they shall sing of the ways of the Lord, for great is the GLORY of the Lord.*

## Grace

**Ephesians 1.7**: *In Him we have redemption through His blood, the forgiveness of our trespasses, according to the riches of His grace.*

## Gifts

**2 Corinthians 9:11**: *You will be enriched in every way to be generous in every way, which through us will produce thanksgiving to God.*

## Now how do you F.E.A.S.T. and Enjoy the 5G Network of GOD?

**F- Focus**: Ask the Holy Spirit to help you focus your mind and heart on HIM alone, removing every distraction. (List your distractions that are preventing you from focusing on HIM)

_______________________________________________

_______________________________________________

______________________________________

______________________________________

**E- Examine** the 5 verses above: Meditate on them. What stands out from these verses to you?

What do you feel God is telling you in these verses? What do they mean to you? Where all have you seen or experienced HIS 5G's today?

______________________________________

______________________________________

______________________________________

______________________________________

**A- Assess** and apply it: Ask the Holy Spirit to give you a deeper revelation of these 5G's. Any attributes of God that strikes you. What does this revelation of HIM do to you? How will you follow through?

______________________________________

______________________________________

______________________________________

______________________________________

**S- Share it**. With every opportunity you get today, tell others. Boast about our God! List who can you tell and what will you tell them.

______________________________________

______________________________________

______________________________________

**T- Thank** and Praise Him for what He has shown you in these verses or around today. Set your mind and heart in an attitude of worship now!

______________________________________

______________________________________

______________________________________

______________________________________

# Day-20

## Goodness
**Psalm 145.9**: *The Lord is good to all, and His mercy is over all that He has made.*

## Greatness
**Jeremiah 32.17:** *Ah Lord GOD! Behold, You have made the heavens and the earth by Your great power and by Your outstretched arm! Nothing is too difficult for You*

## Glory
**Psalms 145.11, 12:** *They shall speak of the GLORY of Your kingdom, and talk of Your power, to make known to the sons of men His mighty acts, and the glorious majesty of His kingdom.*

## Grace
**Ephesians 4.7:** *But grace was given to each one of us according to the measure of Christ's gift.*

## Gifts
**2 Corinthians 9:15:** *Thanks be to God for His inexpressible gift!*

## Now how do you F.E.A.S.T. and Enjoy the 5G Network of GOD?

**F- Focus**: Ask the Holy Spirit to help you focus your mind and heart on HIM alone, removing every distraction. (List your distractions that are preventing you from focusing on HIM)

___________________________________________

___________________________________________

___________________________________________

___________________________________________

**E- Examine** the 5 verses above: Meditate on them. What stands out from these verses to you?

What do you feel God is telling you in these verses? What do they mean to you? Where all have you seen or experienced HIS 5G's today?

_______________________________________________

_______________________________________________

_______________________________________________

_______________________________________________

**A- Assess** and apply it: Ask the Holy Spirit to give you a deeper revelation of these 5G's. Any attributes of God that strikes you. What does this revelation of HIM do to you? How will you follow through?

_______________________________________________

_______________________________________________

_______________________________________________

_______________________________________________

**S- Share it**. With every opportunity you get today, tell others. Boast about our God! List who can you tell and what will you tell them.

_______________________________________________

_______________________________________________

_______________________________________________

_______________________________________________

**T- Thank** and Praise Him for what He has shown you in these verses or around today. Set your mind and heart in an attitude of worship now!

_______________________________________________

_______________________________________________

_______________________________________________

_______________________________________________

# Day-21

## Goodness
**Jeremiah 31.14**: *I will feast the soul of the priests with abundance, and My people shall be satisfied with My goodness, declares the Lord.*

## Greatness
**Nahum 1.3:** *The LORD is slow to anger and great in power....*

## Glory
**Isaiah 4.5:** *Then the Lord will create above every dwelling place of Mount Zion, and above her assemblies, a cloud and smoke by day and the shining of a flaming fire by night. For over all the GLORY there will be a covering.*

## Grace
**Hebrews 2.9**: *But we see Him who for a little while was made lower than the angels, namely Jesus, crowned with glory and honor because of the suffering of death, so that by the grace of God He might taste death for everyone.*

## Gifts
**Galatians 5:22-23**: *But the fruit of the Spirit is love, joy, peace, patience, kindness, goodness, faithfulness, gentleness, self-control; against such things there is no law.*

## Now how do you F.E.A.S.T. and Enjoy the 5G Network of GOD?

**F- Focus**: Ask the Holy Spirit to help you focus your mind and heart on HIM alone, removing every distraction. (List your distractions that are preventing you from focusing on HIM)

_______________________________________________

_______________________________________________

_______________________________________________

_______________________________________________

**E- Examine** the 5 verses above: Meditate on them. What stands out from these verses to you?

What do you feel God is telling you in these verses? What do they mean to you? Where all have you seen or experienced HIS 5G's today?

_______________________________________________

_______________________________________________

_______________________________________________

_______________________________________________

**A- Assess** and apply it: Ask the Holy Spirit to give you a deeper revelation of these 5G's. Any attributes of God that strikes you. What does this revelation of HIM do to you? How will you follow through?

_______________________________________________

_______________________________________________

_______________________________________________

_______________________________________________

**S- Share it**. With every opportunity you get today, tell others. Boast about our God! List who can you tell and what will you tell them.

_______________________________________________

_______________________________________________

_______________________________________________

_______________________________________________

**T- Thank** and Praise Him for what He has shown you in these verses or around today. Set your mind and heart in an attitude of worship now!

_______________________________________________

_______________________________________________

_______________________________________________

# Day-22

### Goodness
**Nahum 1.7**: *The Lord is good, a stronghold in the day of trouble; He knows those who take refuge in Him.*

### Greatness
**Psalms 108.4:** *For Your lovingkindness is great above the heavens, And Your truth reaches to the skies*

### Glory
**Isaiah 6.3:** *And one cried to another and said, "Holy, Holy, Holy, is the Lord of hosts; the whole earth is full of His GLORY!"*

### Grace
**John 1.14**: *And the Word became flesh and dwelt among us, and we have seen His glory, glory as of the only Son from the Father, full of grace and truth.*

### Gifts
**Ephesians 2:8-10**: *For by grace you have been saved through faith. And this is not your own doing; it is the gift of God, not a result of works, so that no one may boast. For we are His workmanship, created in Christ Jesus for good works, which God prepared beforehand, that we should walk in them.*

## Now how do you F.E.A.S.T. and Enjoy the 5G Network of GOD?

**F- Focus**: Ask the Holy Spirit to help you focus your mind and heart on HIM alone, removing every distraction. (List your distractions that are preventing you from focusing on HIM)

_______________________________________________

_______________________________________________

_______________________________________________

_______________________________________________

**E- Examine** the 5 verses above: Meditate on them. What stands out from these verses to you?

What do you feel God is telling you in these verses? What do they mean to you? Where all have you seen or experienced HIS 5G's today?

______________________________________

______________________________________

______________________________________

______________________________________

**A- Assess** and apply it: Ask the Holy Spirit to give you a deeper revelation of these 5G's. Any attributes of God that strikes you. What does this revelation of HIM do to you? How will you follow through?

______________________________________

______________________________________

______________________________________

______________________________________

**S- Share it**. With every opportunity you get today, tell others. Boast about our God! List who can you tell and what will you tell them.

______________________________________

______________________________________

______________________________________

______________________________________

**T- Thank** and Praise Him for what He has shown you in these verses or around today. Set your mind and heart in an attitude of worship now!

______________________________________

______________________________________

______________________________________

______________________________________

# Day-23

## Goodness

**Mark 10.18**: *And Jesus said to him, "Why do you call me good? No one is good except God alone.*

## Greatness

**Psalm 145.3:** *Great is the Lord, and greatly to be praised, and His greatness is unsearchable*

## Glory

**Isaiah 42.8:** *I am the Lord, that is My name; and My GLORY I will not give to another, nor My praise to carved images*

## Grace

**John 1.16**: *And from His fullness we have all received, grace upon grace.*

## Gifts

**Ephesians 4:7-8**: *But grace was given to each one of us according to the measure of Christ's gift. Therefore it says, "When He ascended on high He led a host of captives, and He gave gifts to men."*

## Now how do you F.E.A.S.T. and Enjoy the 5G Network of GOD?

**F- Focus**: Ask the Holy Spirit to help you focus your mind and heart on HIM alone, removing every distraction. (List your distractions that are preventing you from focusing on HIM)

_______________________________________________

_______________________________________________

_______________________________________________

_______________________________________________

**E- Examine** the 5 verses above: Meditate on them. What stands out from these verses to you?

What do you feel God is telling you in these verses? What do they mean to you? Where all have you seen or experienced HIS 5G's today?

__________________________________________

__________________________________________

__________________________________________

__________________________________________

**A- Assess** and apply it: Ask the Holy Spirit to give you a deeper revelation of these 5G's. Any attributes of God that strikes you. What does this revelation of HIM do to you? How will you follow through?

__________________________________________

__________________________________________

__________________________________________

__________________________________________

**S- Share it**. With every opportunity you get today, tell others. Boast about our God! List who can you tell and what will you tell them.

__________________________________________

__________________________________________

__________________________________________

__________________________________________

**T- Thank** and Praise Him for what He has shown you in these verses or around today. Set your mind and heart in an attitude of worship now!

__________________________________________

__________________________________________

__________________________________________

__________________________________________

# Day-24

## Goodness

**Luke 11.13**: *If you then, who are evil, know how to give good gifts to your children, how much more will the heavenly Father give the Holy Spirit to those who ask Him!*

## Greatness

**Matthew 12.6:** *But I say to you that something greater than the temple is here.*

## Glory

**Isaiah 59.19:** *So shall they fear the name of the Lord from the west, and His GLORY from the rising of the sun; when the enemy comes in, like a flood the Spirit of the Lord will lift up a standard against him.*

## Grace

**John 1.17**: *For the law was given through Moses; grace and truth came through Jesus Christ.*

## Gifts

**Colossians 3:23-24**: *Whatever you do, work heartily, as for the Lord and not for men, knowing that from the Lord you will receive the inheritance as your reward. You are serving the Lord Christ.*

## Now how do you F.E.A.S.T. and Enjoy the 5G Network of GOD?

**F- Focus**: Ask the Holy Spirit to help you focus your mind and heart on HIM alone, removing every distraction. (List your distractions that are preventing you from focusing on HIM)

_______________________________________________

_______________________________________________

_______________________________________________

**E- Examine** the 5 verses above: Meditate on them. What stands out from these verses to you?

What do you feel God is telling you in these verses? What do they mean to you? Where all have you seen or experienced HIS 5G's today?

_______________________________________________

_______________________________________________

_______________________________________________

_______________________________________________

**A- Assess** and apply it: Ask the Holy Spirit to give you a deeper revelation of these 5G's. Any attributes of God that strikes you. What does this revelation of HIM do to you? How will you follow through?

_______________________________________________

_______________________________________________

_______________________________________________

_______________________________________________

**S- Share it**. With every opportunity you get today, tell others. Boast about our God! List who can you tell and what will you tell them.

_______________________________________________

_______________________________________________

_______________________________________________

_______________________________________________

**T- Thank** and Praise Him for what He has shown you in these verses or around today. Set your mind and heart in an attitude of worship now!

_______________________________________________

_______________________________________________

_______________________________________________

_______________________________________________

# Day-25

## Goodness

**Acts 10.38:** *How God anointed Jesus of Nazareth with the Holy Spirit and with power. He went about doing good and healing all who were oppressed by the devil, for God was with Him.*

## Greatness

**Psalm 126.3:** *The LORD has done great things for us; We are glad.*

## Glory

**Isaiah 60.1, 2:** *Arise, shine; for your light has come! And the GLORY of the Lord is risen upon you. For behold, the darkness shall cover the earth, and deep darkness the people; but the Lord will arise over you, and His GLORY will be seen upon you.*

## Grace

**Romans 3.24**: *And are justified by His grace as a gift, through the redemption that is in Christ Jesus.*

## Gifts

**1 Timothy 4:14**: *Do not neglect the gift you have, which was given to you by prophecy when the council of elders laid their hands on you.*

## Now how do you F.E.A.S.T. and Enjoy the 5G Network of GOD?

**F- Focus**: Ask the Holy Spirit to help you focus your mind and heart on HIM alone, removing every distraction. (List your distractions that are preventing you from focusing on HIM)

_______________________________________________

_______________________________________________

_______________________________________________

_______________________________________________

**E- Examine** the 5 verses above: Meditate on them. What stands out from these verses to you?

What do you feel God is telling you in these verses? What do they mean to you? Where all have you seen or experienced HIS 5G's today?

_______________________________________________

_______________________________________________

_______________________________________________

_______________________________________________

**A- Assess** and apply it: Ask the Holy Spirit to give you a deeper revelation of these 5G's. Any attributes of God that strikes you. What does this revelation of HIM do to you? How will you follow through?

_______________________________________________

_______________________________________________

_______________________________________________

_______________________________________________

**S- Share it**. With every opportunity you get today, tell others. Boast about our God! List who can you tell and what will you tell them.

_______________________________________________

_______________________________________________

_______________________________________________

_______________________________________________

**T- Thank** and Praise Him for what He has shown you in these verses or around today. Set your mind and heart in an attitude of worship now!

_______________________________________________

_______________________________________________

_______________________________________________

_______________________________________________

# Day-26

## Goodness

**Acts 14.17**: *Yet He did not leave himself without witness, for He did good by giving you rains from heaven and fruitful seasons, satisfying your hearts with food and gladness.*

## Greatness

**Psalm 126.2:** *"Then our mouth was filled with laughter And our tongue with joyful shouting; Then they said among the nations, "The LORD has done great things for them."*

## Glory

**Isaiah 62.3:** *You shall be a crown of GLORY in the hand of the Lord, and a royal diadem in the hand of your God.*

## Grace

**Romans 5.15**: *But the free gift is not like the trespass. For if many died through one man's trespass, much more have the grace of God and the free gift by the grace of that one man Jesus Christ abounded for many.*

## Gifts

**2 Timothy 1:6-7**: *For this reason I remind you to fan into flame the gift of God, which is in you through the laying on of my hands, for God gave us a spirit not of fear but of power and love and self-control.*

## Now how do you F.E.A.S.T. and Enjoy the 5G Network of GOD?

**F- Focus**: Ask the Holy Spirit to help you focus your mind and heart on HIM alone, removing every distraction. (List your distractions that are preventing you from focusing on HIM)

_______________________________________________

_______________________________________________

_______________________________________________

_______________________________________________

**E- Examine** the 5 verses above: Meditate on them. What stands out from these verses to you?

What do you feel God is telling you in these verses? What do they mean to you? Where all have you seen or experienced HIS 5G's today?

_______________________________________________

_______________________________________________

_______________________________________________

_______________________________________________

**A- Assess** and apply it: Ask the Holy Spirit to give you a deeper revelation of these 5G's. Any attributes of God that strikes you. What does this revelation of HIM do to you? How will you follow through?

_______________________________________________

_______________________________________________

_______________________________________________

_______________________________________________

**S- Share it**. With every opportunity you get today, tell others. Boast about our God! List who can you tell and what will you tell them.

_______________________________________________

_______________________________________________

_______________________________________________

_______________________________________________

**T- Thank** and Praise Him for what He has shown you in these verses or around today. Set your mind and heart in an attitude of worship now!

_______________________________________________

_______________________________________________

_______________________________________________

_______________________________________________

# Day-27

### Goodness
**Galatians 5.22-23**: *But the fruit of the Spirit is love, joy, peace, patience, kindness, goodness, faithfulness, gentleness, self-control; against such things there is no law.*

### Greatness
**Jeremiah 32.18:** *...Who shows lovingkindness to thousands, but repays the iniquity of fathers into the bosom of their children after them, O great and mighty God The LORD of hosts is His name;*

### Glory
**Ezekiel 8.4:** *And behold, the GLORY of the God of Israel was there, like the vision that I saw in the plain.*

### Grace
**Romans 5.17**: *For if, because of one man's trespass, death reigned through that one man, much more will those who receive the abundance of grace and the free gift of righteousness reign in life through the one man Jesus Christ.*

### Gifts
**Hebrews 2:4**: *While God also bore witness by signs and wonders and various miracles and by gifts of the Holy Spirit distributed according to His will.*

**Now how do you F.E.A.S.T. and Enjoy the 5G Network of GOD?**

**F- Focus**: Ask the Holy Spirit to help you focus your mind and heart on HIM alone, removing every distraction. (List your distractions that are preventing you from focusing on HIM)

_______________________________________

_______________________________________

_______________________________________

_______________________________________

**E- Examine** the 5 verses above: Meditate on them. What stands out from these verses to you?

What do you feel God is telling you in these verses? What do they mean to you? Where all have you seen or experienced HIS 5G's today?

_______________________________________________

_______________________________________________

_______________________________________________

_______________________________________________

**A- Assess** and apply it: Ask the Holy Spirit to give you a deeper revelation of these 5G's. Any attributes of God that strikes you. What does this revelation of HIM do to you? How will you follow through?

_______________________________________________

_______________________________________________

_______________________________________________

_______________________________________________

**S- Share it**. With every opportunity you get today, tell others. Boast about our God! List who can you tell and what will you tell them.

_______________________________________________

_______________________________________________

_______________________________________________

_______________________________________________

**T- Thank** and Praise Him for what He has shown you in these verses or around today. Set your mind and heart in an attitude of worship now!

_______________________________________________

_______________________________________________

_______________________________________________

# Day-28

## Goodness

**Ephesians 2.10**: *For we are His workmanship, created in Christ Jesus for good works, which God prepared beforehand, that we should walk in them.*

## Greatness

**Deuteronomy 3.24:** *O Lord GOD, You have begun to show Your servant Your greatness and Your strong hand; for what god is there in heaven or on earth who can do such works and mighty acts as Yours?*

## Glory

**Ezekiel 9.3:** *Now the GLORY of the God of Israel had gone up from the Cherub, where it had been, to the threshold of the temple. And he called to the man clothed with linen, who had the writer's inkhorn at his side.*

## Grace

**Romans 5.20**: *Now the law came in to increase the trespass, but where sin increased, grace abounded all the more.*

## Gifts

**James 1:5**: *If any of you lacks wisdom, let him ask God, who gives generously to all without reproach, and it will be given him.*

**Now how do you F.E.A.S.T. and Enjoy the 5G Network of GOD?**

**F- Focus**: Ask the Holy Spirit to help you focus your mind and heart on HIM alone, removing every distraction. (List your distractions that are preventing you from focusing on HIM)

_______________________________________________

_______________________________________________

_______________________________________________

_______________________________________________

**E- Examine** the 5 verses above: Meditate on them. What stands out from these verses to you?

What do you feel God is telling you in these verses? What do they mean to you? Where all have you seen or experienced HIS 5G's today?

_______________________________________________

_______________________________________________

_______________________________________________

_______________________________________________

**A- Assess** and apply it: Ask the Holy Spirit to give you a deeper revelation of these 5G's. Any attributes of God that strikes you. What does this revelation of HIM do to you? How will you follow through?

_______________________________________________

_______________________________________________

_______________________________________________

_______________________________________________

**S- Share it**. With every opportunity you get today, tell others. Boast about our God! List who can you tell and what will you tell them.

_______________________________________________

_______________________________________________

_______________________________________________

_______________________________________________

**T- Thank** and Praise Him for what He has shown you in these verses or around today. Set your mind and heart in an attitude of worship now!

_______________________________________________

_______________________________________________

_______________________________________________

_______________________________________________

# Day-29

### Goodness
**Philippians 1.6**: *And I am sure of this, that He who began a good work in you will bring it to completion at the day of Jesus Christ.*

### Greatness
**Psalm 77.13:** *Your way, O God, is holy; What god is great like our God?*

### Glory
**Ezekiel 10.19:** *And the cherubim lifted their wings and mounted up from the earth in my sight. When they went out, the wheels were beside them; and they stood at the door of the east gate of the Lord's house, and the GLORY of the God of Israel was above them.*

### Grace
**Romans 5.21**: *So that, as sin reigned in death, grace also might reign through righteousness leading to eternal life through Jesus Christ our Lord.*

### Gifts
**1 Peter 4:10:** *As each has received a gift, use it to serve one another, as good stewards of God's varied grace:*

### Now how do you F.E.A.S.T. and Enjoy the 5G Network of GOD?

F- Focus: Ask the Holy Spirit to help you focus your mind and heart on HIM alone, removing every distraction. (List your distractions that are preventing you from focusing on HIM)

_______________________________________________

_______________________________________________

_______________________________________________

_______________________________________________

**E- Examine** the 5 verses above: Meditate on them. What stands out from these verses to you?

What do you feel God is telling you in these verses? What do they mean to you? Where all have you seen or experienced HIS 5G's today?

_______________________________________________

_______________________________________________

_______________________________________________

_______________________________________________

**A- Assess** and apply it: Ask the Holy Spirit to give you a deeper revelation of these 5G's. Any attributes of God that strikes you. What does this revelation of HIM do to you? How will you follow through?

_______________________________________________

_______________________________________________

_______________________________________________

_______________________________________________

**S- Share it**. With every opportunity you get today, tell others. Boast about our God! List who can you tell and what will you tell them.

_______________________________________________

_______________________________________________

_______________________________________________

_______________________________________________

**T- Thank** and Praise Him for what He has shown you in these verses or around today. Set your mind and heart in an attitude of worship now!

_______________________________________________

_______________________________________________

_______________________________________________

_______________________________________________

# Day-30

## Goodness
**1 Timothy 4.4**: *For everything created by God is good, and nothing is to be rejected if it is received with thanksgiving.*

## Greatness
**Psalm 95.3***: For the LORD is a great God And a great King above all gods*

## Glory
**Ezekiel 43.1-5:** *"Afterward he brought me to the gate, the gate that faces toward the east. And behold, the GLORY of the God of Israel came from the way of the east. His voice was like the sound of many waters; and the earth shone with His GLORY. It was like the appearance of the vision which I saw—like the vision which I saw when I came to destroy the city. The visions were like the vision which I saw by the River Chebar; and I fell on my face. And the GLORY of the LORD came into the temple by way of the gate which faces toward the east. The Spirit lifted me up and brought me into the inner court; and behold, the GLORY of the LORD filled the temple."*

## Grace
**Romans 6.14**: *For sin will have no dominion over you, since you are not under law but under grace.*

## Gifts
**1 John 5:15**: *And if we know that He hears us in whatever we ask, we know that we have the requests that we have asked of Him.*

## Now how do you F.E.A.S.T. and Enjoy the 5G Network of GOD?

**F- Focus**: Ask the Holy Spirit to help you focus your mind and heart on HIM alone, removing every distraction. (List your distractions that are preventing you from focusing on HIM)

_______________________________________________

_______________________________________________

___________________________________________

___________________________________________

**E- Examine** the 5 verses above: Meditate on them. What stands out from these verses to you?

What do you feel God is telling you in these verses? What do they mean to you? Where all have you seen or experienced HIS 5G's today?

___________________________________________

___________________________________________

___________________________________________

___________________________________________

**A- Assess** and apply it: Ask the Holy Spirit to give you a deeper revelation of these 5G's. Any attributes of God that strikes you. What does this revelation of HIM do to you? How will you follow through?

___________________________________________

___________________________________________

___________________________________________

___________________________________________

**S- Share it**. With every opportunity you get today, tell others. Boast about our God! List who can you tell and what will you tell them.

___________________________________________

___________________________________________

___________________________________________

___________________________________________

**T- Thank** and Praise Him for what He has shown you in these verses or around today. Set your mind and heart in an attitude of worship now!

___________________________________________

___________________________________________

___________________________________________

___________________________________________

# Day-31

## Goodness

**James 1.17**: *Every good gift and every perfect gift is from above, coming down from the Father of lights with whom there is no variation or shadow due to change.*

## Greatness

**Psalm 86.8-10:** *There is none like You among the gods, O Lord, nor are there any works like Yours. All the nations You have made shall come and worship before You, O Lord, and shall glorify Your name. For You are great and do wondrous things; You alone are God*

## Glory

**Psalm 29.3**: *"The voice of the LORD is upon the waters; The God of GLORY thunders, The LORD is over many waters."*

## Grace

**Titus 3.7**: *So that being justified by His grace we might become heirs according to the hope of eternal life.*

## Gifts

**Revelation 22:17**: *The Spirit and the Bride say, "Come." And let the one who hears say, "Come." And let the one who is thirsty come; let the one who desires take the water of life without price.*

## Now how do you F.E.A.S.T. and Enjoy the 5G Network of GOD?

**F- Focus**: Ask the Holy Spirit to help you focus your mind and heart on HIM alone, removing every distraction. (List your distractions that are preventing you from focusing on HIM)

_______________________________________________
_______________________________________________
_______________________________________________
_______________________________________________

**E- Examine** the 5 verses above: Meditate on them. What stands out from these verses to you?

What do you feel God is telling you in these verses? What do they mean to you? Where all have you seen or experienced HIS 5G's today?

_______________________________________________

_______________________________________________

_______________________________________________

_______________________________________________

**A- Assess** and apply it: Ask the Holy Spirit to give you a deeper revelation of these 5G's. Any attributes of God that strikes you. What does this revelation of HIM do to you? How will you follow through?

_______________________________________________

_______________________________________________

_______________________________________________

_______________________________________________

**S- Share it**. With every opportunity you get today, tell others. Boast about our God! List who can you tell and what will you tell them.

_______________________________________________

_______________________________________________

_______________________________________________

_______________________________________________

**T- Thank** and Praise Him for what He has shown you in these verses or around today. Set your mind and heart in an attitude of worship now!

_______________________________________________

_______________________________________________

_______________________________________________

_______________________________________________

# About the Author

**Gerard Assey**, pastors a growing church: **'Throne Room Worship'**- an avenue for God's children to come together and give HIM the only food that He enjoys - 'PRAISE AND WORSHIP'. As a layman, Gerard is Chief Executive of the group: 'Citius, Altius, Fortius Unlimited'- a successful training organization, serving some of the topmost names worldwide.

Pastor Gerard has also for over 9 years served as a Part-time Faculty at the Charis Bible College-Chennai (Andrew Wommack Ministries-Colorado, USA), for sessions on 'Presentation & Preaching Skills' along with 'Biblical Leadership Skills and Other Trainings'. He has also been on the board of a few international organizations – The Vine Charitable Trust (Part of 'Anglo-Indian Concern'-UK), People of the Way Fellowship and for a few years on the board as past Managing Trustee of the Andrew Wommack Ministries-India, to name some.

An author of 4 published secular books:

1. Bite-sized Bits on Commonsense Management

2. Heart to Heart on Life's Principles'

3. How to become a Successful Manager

4. The Sales Professionals' Master Workbook of S.Y.S.T.E.M.S

…And his most recent Christian Books being:

1.   'A Bouquet of Praises for My KING',

2.   Christian Jokes for the Serious Religious' Folks!

3.   Jesus Healed You!

Gerard has also produced a CD titled: **HE HEALS TODAY!** - A subject very close to his heart, and made available free of charge on website: www.JesusHealedYou.com.

Finally, Gerard is the SON of the MOST HIGH GOD, a Husband to a beautiful wife, June of 35 years, a Father of Four (a daughter and a son & their respective partners), Grandfather of 3 kings and a beautiful Princess, Pastor & Preacher, Author, Business Management Consultant, Corporate Trainer, Voice Over Artist & here's the best title…a Worshipper!

*Gerard is an ordinary guy following an extraordinary God!*

# More from us!

Also, you might like to have a look at our other books available:

https://www.amazon.com/s?k=gerard+assey&ref=nb_sb_noss_1


Please visit our websites too:

www.PreachingSkills.com

www.JesusHealedYou.com

www.ChristianMinistryTraining.com